EX LIBRIS

Bill Howell

SILVER SCREEN COWBOYS

ROBERT PHILLIPS

SALT LAKE CITY

97 96 95 94 93   10 9 8 7 6 5 4 3 2 1

Text © 1993 by Robert W. Phillips

Published by Gibbs Smith, Publisher
Peregrine Smith Books
P.O. Box 667, Layton, Utah 84041

Printed in Hong Kong

Cover and interior design by Warren Archer II
Lynda Sessions Sorenson, Editor
Dawn Valentine, Editorial Assistant

Photography Credits:
Buffalo Bill Cody – Culver Pictures
Clayton Moore – © Lone Ranger Television, Inc.
All otherwise not noted: Phillips Archives

Library of Congress Cataloging-in-Publication Data
Phillips, Robert
        Silver Screen cowboys / Robert Phillips
            p.   cm.
        ISBN 0-87905-578-2
        1. Western films – Miscellanea. 2. Motion picture actors and actresses – United
    States – Miscellanea. 3. Television actors and actresses – United States –
    Miscellanea I. Title.
PN1995.9.W4P47   1993
791 . 43'6278 – dc20   93 – 14070
                                                                              CIP

❖ The Silver Screen Cowboys ❖

The heroes that truly caught the imagination of a young country and made opening up the western frontier sound daring and glamourous were the cowboys. While cowboys were once only low-paid laborers punching cattle across the Southwest, early filmmakers and novelists cultivated and civilized the cowboy image, and it spread like a prairie fire through every aspect of American culture. Not surprisingly, as silent movies turned to talkies and talkies turned to television, the classic American hero remained the cowboy.

❖ BUFFALO BILL CODY ❖

1846-1917

CREATING AND CULTIVATING
THE IMAGE OF THE DARING AND ROMANTIC
AMERICAN COWBOY WAS HELPED ALONG BY EARLY
SHOW PERFORMERS SUCH AS BUFFALO BILL CODY. BORN AS
WILLIAM F. CODY, ON FEBRUARY 26, 1846, IN IOWA, HE WAS
AN INDIAN FIGHTER AND A SCOUT BEFORE LAUNCHING A SHOW-
BUSINESS CAREER. HIS FAMOUS SHOW, "BUFFALO BILL'S WILD
WEST," EMPLOYED SUCH NOTABLES AS ANNIE OAKLEY
AND CHIEF SITTING BULL AND SET THE STAGE
FOR THE LATER APPEARANCE OF THE
MUCH-LOVED SILVER SCREEN
COWBOYS.

❖ William S. Hart ❖

Born on December 6, 1865,
in Newburgh, New York. His acquaintance
with real cowboys and Indians spurred his decision
to play the part of the cowboy in almost all of his
sixty-nine films. According to him, "a real
cowboy doesn't smile," and he rarely
did. He ruled the range
from 1915 to 1925.
He died in 1946.

❖ Tom Mix ❖

Born January 6, 1880,
in Mix Run, Pennsylvania.
Tom went from skilled rider to Texas Ranger,
to rodeo champion in "Miller Brothers Wild West
Show." Our sagebrush hero then began a
legendary film career. Tom and
his horse, Tony, saddled up
for nearly three hundred
silver screen sagas. He
died in 1940.

❖ TIM McCOY ❖

BORN APRIL 10, 1891,
IN SAGINAW, MICHIGAN. HE WAS A WYOMING
RANCHER AND AN INDIAN AGENT, HE BEGAN HIS FILM
CAREER AS A TECHNICAL ADVISOR. HE WAS THE HERO OF THE
FIRST SOUND SERIAL AT UNIVERSAL STUDIOS AND IS CREDITED
WITH BEING A TRICK RIDER IN *THE COVERED WAGON*
(1923). HE WAS ONE OF HOLLYWOOD'S MOST
POPULAR WESTERN STARS WHO MADE
MORE THAN SEVENTY FILMS.
HE DIED IN 1978.

❖ BUCK JONES ❖

BORN DECEMBER 12, 1891, IN VINCENNES,
INDIANA, AS CHARLES FREDERICK GEBHART. HE WAS
AN EXPERT HORSEMAN EVEN AS A CHILD. HE SERVED IN
THE U.S. ARMY AS PART OF THE SIXTH CAVALRY, SEEING
ACTION IN MEXICO AND THE PHILLIPINES. THIS EXPERIENCE
PROMPTED A STINT IN WILD WEST SHOWS AND CIRCUSES, AND
THEN A HOLLYWOOD DEBUT. AN EXTRA, A STUNTMAN AND A
STAR, HE JINGLED HIS SPURS AND RODE HIS HORSE, SILVER,
IN JUST UNDER 150 TUMBLEWEED TALES. HIS BRILLIANT
CAREER WAS CUT SHORT IN A FIRE IN THE COCOANUT
GROVE CLUB IN BOSTON IN 1942, WHEN BUCK
PERISHED—A REAL LIFE HERO, WHILE
TRYING TO RESCUE PEOPLE
CAUGHT IN THE FIRE.

❖ Ken Maynard ❖

Born July 21, 1895,
in Vevay, Indiana. Ken was a trick rider
and a rodeo champion who rode with Buffalo
Bill and Ringling Brothers, until his film debut in 1924.
After having made more than fifty movies and
the popular Trail Blazer serials, he
retired in the 1940s, making
only brief appearances for
his adoring public.
He died in 1973.

❖ Gene Autry ❖

Born September 29, 1907,
in Tioga, Texas. He was a railroad
telegrapher with a gold-plated voice.
Humorist Will Rogers convinced Autry to try his
luck at warbling on the radio. His illustrious film career
began in 1934, following success in radio and recording.
He became known as "America's Favorite Singing
Cowboy," and the "World's Greatest Cowboy."
He thrilled his many fans with more
than ninety action-packed,
silver-screen escapades,
astride his horse,
Champion.

❖ TEX RITTER ❖

BORN ON JANUARY 12, 1905,
IN MURVAUL, TEXAS. TEX BECAME KNOWN AS
"AMERICA'S MOST BELOVED COWBOY." WITH A GUITAR,
HIS PISTOLS AND HIS SONGS, HE RODE HIS HORSE, WHITE FLASH,
TO CHASE THE BAD GUYS OUT OF THE WEST IN MORE
THAN FIFTY FILMS. HE ATTAINED SPECIAL FAME
FOR SINGING THE THEME SONG
IN THE FILM *HIGH NOON*.
HE DIED IN 1974.

❖ WILLIAM BOYD ❖

BORN ON JUNE 5, 1898, IN
CAMBRIDGE, OHIO. AS HOPALONG CASSIDY
HE DRESSED IN BLACK AND RODE A SNOW WHITE
HORSE NAMED TOPPER. "HOPPY" THRILLED MILLIONS
OF CHILDREN AS HE CHAMPIONED JUSTICE AND
TAUGHT ALL OF US TO BE GOOD, HONEST
AMERICANS. HE MADE MORE THAN
SIXTY-FIVE FILMS FROM 1935 TO
1948 AND DIED IN 1972.

❖ Roy Rogers ❖

Born November 5, 1911,
in Cincinnati, Ohio, as Leonard Sly.
The "King of the Cowboys" blazed the trail
on his golden palomino, Trigger, the "Smartest
Horse in the Movies." With his guitar in hand, and
pistols on his hips, he sang and chased the villains
from the scene through nearly a hundred movies.
Later with his faithful dog, Bullet, his wife, Dale
Evans and sidekick, Pat Brady, he punched
out the bad guys in more than
one hundred TV episodes.

❖ ROCKY LANE ❖

BORN SEPTEMBER 22, 1904,
IN MISHAWAKA, INDIANA, AS HAROLD ALBERSHART.
THIS CLEAN-CUT WESTERN STAR OF THE 1940S HAD BAD MEN
SHAKING IN THEIR BOOTS WHEN HE AND HIS WONDER HORSE,
BLACK JACK, MADE THE STREETS OF THE OLD WEST SAFE
FOR WOMEN AND CHILDREN DURING MORE THAN
ONE HUNDRED FILMS AND SERIALS. ROCKY
BECAME THE VOICE OF MR. ED IN
THE TV SERIES OF THE SIXTIES.
HE DIED IN 1973.

❖ Monte Hale ❖

Born June 8, 1921,
in San Angelo, Texas. Hale
was a singer by age twelve. He went on to
become the easy-going cowboy who was groomed
to take Roy Rogers' place if Roy was drafted. He found
a special place of his own in the hearts of children
while riding the dusty trails on his horse, Pardner,
in fancy attire often rivaling that of
Roy Rogers. He tried to avoid the title
"Singing cowboy" and, in his
twenty-nine starring
roles, sang only
occasionally.

❖ Lash LaRue ❖

Born either June 15, 1917,
or March 5, 1921 (he preferred not to say),
in either Michigan or Gretna, Louisiana (again he
wouldn't say), as Alfred LaRue. Strong, silent, dressed in
black, sporting a fifteen-foot black bullwhip and
riding Black Diamond, he terrorized outlaws
and protected ladies and children.
He rarely used his gun in any of
his twenty-four films.

❖ Clayton Moore as ❖ The Lone Ranger©

Born on
September 14, 1914,
in Chicago, Illinois. Often
mistaken for an outlaw because of
the mask, this lone Texas Ranger was always
on the side of law and justice. The bad guys quivered
from their jail cells and queried, "Who was
that masked man?" as he rode across
our TV screens shouting a
hearty "Hi Yo Silver."

❖ CHARLES STARRETT ❖ AKA THE DURANGO KID

BORN MARCH 28, 1903,
IN ATHOL, MASSACHUSETTS. THIS TWO-FISTED,
GUN-SLINGING, WHITE-HATTED, MINION OF JUSTICE RODE
HIS WHITE HORSE, RAIDER, ACROSS THE SCREEN IN MORE
THAN 130 B-WESTERNS. HE WAS STILL THE
GOOD GUY, JUST WEARING A BLACK HAT, IN
THE "DURANGO KID" SERIES.
HE DIED IN 1986.

❖ Randolph Scott ❖

Born January 23, 1903,
in Orange County, Virginia. He
plucked our heart strings and stirred
our imaginations whether he played the good
guy or the bad guy. This craggy-faced, soft-spoken
cowboy led us down the trails of the Old
West and made us believe we were
right there with him, in more
than sixty western movies.
He died in 1987.

❖ GARY COOPER ❖

Born May 7, 1901,
in Helena, Montana. The tall, lanky
cowboy was most memorable as he stood alone
to face the bad guys. His image was that of the strong,
silent, no-nonsense marshal that we knew and
loved, as witnessed in his Oscar-winning
performance in *High Noon*,
in 1952. Gary Cooper
died in 1961.

❖ Hugh O'Brian ❖

Born April 19, 1925,
in Rochester, New York.
After a stint as one of the youngest
Marine Drill Instructors in World War II,
he perpetuated the "brave courageous, and bold"
image of the legendary, snappily dressed,
gunfighting, Marshal
Wyatt Earp, on TV
in the 1950s.

❖ George Montgomery ❖

Born August 29, 1916,
in Brady, Montana. Using
his real name, George Letz, he began
his acting career in 1935 as a stuntman for
Republic Pictures. In the 1940s he became a star of
western movies as George Montgomery.
This masculine, rugged he-man
personified the image of
the American cowboy.

❖ Joel McCrea ❖

Born November 5, 1905,
in Los Angeles, California. He was
one of the last actors to enter a movie
career in the silent-screen era. This good-
looking, steady, dependable, always-cool cowboy
was loved by millions, including his producers and
directors, for his modest, good-natured personality.
After the mid 1940s, he remained a star, rarely
deviating from the western genre.
He died in 1990.

❖ John Wayne ❖

Born on
May 26, 1907, in
Winterset, Iowa, as Michael
Marion Morrison. He went from
B-westerns to high-budget films. "The Duke"
dedicated his life to representing the great American
hero, projecting a 6-foot 4-inch legend. Every boy
wanted to be him, and every girl wanted
to marry him. Even since his death in
1979, his legend has continued
to grow, as always,
larger than life.

❖ Morgan Woodward ❖

Born September 16, 1925,
in Arlington, Texas. A formidable giant
of a man, he lent his rugged western features to
scores of character roles in many of our most memorable
cowboy films, in addition to many "Gunsmoke" TV
episodes. He played both the good guy and
the bad guy, but in either role, he was
as tough as his boots and hard-
headed enough to intimidate
his adversary.

❖ ABOUT THE AUTHOR ❖

ROBERT W. PHILLIPS, AUTHOR, EDITOR AND RESEARCHER, IS A NATIVE TEXAN, WHO GREW UP ON RODEOS, PARADES AND HONKY-TONKS. HIS INTEREST IN WESTERN AMERICANA GREW OUT OF HIS BOYHOOD EXPERIENCES AND FROM WATCHING "HOPPY, GENE AND ROY" CHASE THE BAD GUYS ACROSS THE SILVER SCREEN. HE HAS COLLECTED AND RESEARCHED MEMORABILIA, CONNECTED WITH THE AMERICAN COWBOY HEROES OF FILM AND TELEVISION, FOR OVER THIRTY YEARS. HE IS A RECOGNIZED AUTHORITY ON ROY ROGERS AND BOB WILLS AND HIS HUGE REFERENCE BOOK ON ROGERS IS SCHEDULED FOR RELEASE IN 1994. HIS EXPERTISE HAS BROUGHT HIM NUMEROUS BOOKS, UNDER CONTRACT TO TWO PUBLISHERS, SCREEN CREDITS—AS A RESEARCH CONSULTANT AND MANY PUBLISHED MAGAZINE ARTICLES. IN ADDITION TO HIS RESEARCH ON SILVER SCREEN HEROES, PHILLIPS IS RESPONSIBLE FOR MUCH PIONEERING STUDY OF THE DELL WESTERN COWBOY COMIC BOOKS OF THE 1940S-1960S. HE IS ON THE COMICS SCHOLARS LIST OF MICHIGAN STATE UNIVERSITY AND CURRENTLY PUBLISHES *WESTERN COMICS JOURNAL*, A JOURNAL DEVOTED TO SCHOLARLY RESEARCH OF THE WESTERN COMIC BOOK MEDIUM. TO BE CLOSER TO PUBLISHERS AND FILM PRODUCERS, HE NOW LIVES IN NEW YORK CITY WHERE HE IS CURRENTLY RESEARCHING THAT CITY'S ROLE IN POPULARIZING THE COWBOY.